MOAT HALL P
JOHN'S LANE,
GREAT WYRLE
WALSALL, WS

My First ACROSTIC

Poems From The Midlands

Edited by Jenni Bannister

First published in Great Britain in 2015 by:

Young Writers

Remus House
Coltsfoot Drive
Peterborough
PE2 9BF
Telephone: 01733 890066
Website: www.youngwriters.co.uk

All Rights Reserved
Book Design by Ashley Janson
© Copyright Contributors 2015
ISBN 978-1-78443-587-5

Printed and bound in the UK by BookPrintingUK
Website: www.bookprintinguk.com

FOREWORD

Welcome, Reader!

For Young Writers' latest competition, My First Acrostic, we gave Key Stage 1 children nationwide the challenge of writing an acrostic poem on the topic of their choice.

Poetry is a wonderful way to introduce young children to the idea of rhyme and rhythm and helps learning and development of communication, language and literacy skills. The acrostic form is a great introduction to poetry, giving a simple framework for pupils to structure their thoughts while at the same time allowing more confident writers the freedom to let their imaginations run wild.

Here at Young Writers our aim is to encourage creativity in children and to inspire a love of the written word, so it's great to get such an amazing response, with some absolutely fantastic poems. This made it a tough challenge to pick the winners, so well done to **Saxon Nicholls** who has been chosen as the best poet in this anthology.

Due to the young age of the entrants we have tried to include as many of the poems as possible. By giving these young poets the chance to see their work in print we hope to encourage their love of poetry and give them the confidence to continue with their creative efforts – I look forward to reading more of their poems in the future.

Jenni Bannister
Editorial Manager

CONTENTS

Ryan Patra (5) 1

Ball Green Primary School, Stoke-On-Trent
Caitlin Shirley Brown (5) 1
Tafira Enock Sambizi (6) 2
Ruby Bourne (6) 2
Mackenzie Oxley (7) 3
Lillie-Mae McCue (7) 3
Jarome Moston (6) 4
Lakelyn Jordan (7) 4
Mitchell Sturgess (6) 5
Lucy Marie Phillips (7) 5
Britton McKhai Leese (7) 6
Elsie Kamili (7) 6
Millie Richards-Snape (7) 7
Summer Lea (6) 7
Camron Ford (7) 8
Ella Daley (7) 8
Antonia Meredith (6) 9
Maxwell Mongo (7) 9
Leah Key (6) 10
Tye Daniel Terry-Jones (6) 10
Jaiden Richardson (7) 11
Everlyn Catherine Peake (6) 11
Demi-Jo Bailey 12
Chloe Kirk (6) 12
Matthew Pritchard (5) 13
Conner Robinson (6) 13
Brogan Michael Leese (6) 14
Dylan 14
Abi 15
Louie Hughes 15
Matthew Russell Pritchard (5) 16
Bailee 16
Demi Bowers 17
Kaitlyn Skye Davies (6) 17
Maddie May Lucas (6) 18
Keira Upton 18
Ella Lyons 19

Brookside Primary School, Leicester
Mikail Asim Ahmed Siddiqui (7) 19
Linda Sun (6) 20
Emelia Bray (5) 21
Muhammad Jagot (6) 22
Devan Kakkad (6) 23
Arooj Rizwan Khatri (6) 24
Darsh Balasubramaniam (6) 25
Mohammed-Hussain Patel (6) 25
Mustafa Ahmed Lafta Alhindawe (5) 26
Sehrish Malik (5) 26
Layla Moonen-Patel (7) 27
Ikjot Kaur Sandhu (5) 27
Anum Hussain (7) 28

Granby Primary School, Leicester
Miller Sweet (5) 28
Szymon Serwicki (7) 29
Tia Grace Burke (6) 29
Jed Whittal-Williams (7) 30
Freya Kate Boniface (6) 30
Leah Halford-Jones (6) 31
Jaydan James Whitmore (5) 31
Arianit Xhylani 32
Joe Kiggell (6) 32
Saxon Nicholls (6) 33
Emmie Noon (6) 33
Ananya Gulati (6) 34
Maximillian Brown (7) 34
Amber Kaur Supria (6) 35
Krish Sookye (7) 35
Alfie Snow (5) 36
Joshua Marvell 36
Theo Dixon (6) 37
Lexi Smales (5) 37
Mia Bayle-Kuhn (6) 38

Greens Norton CE Primary School, Towcester

Megan Connie Brightman (7) 38
Samuel Miller (5) 39
Charlie Bottomley (7) 39
Andrew Doig (6) 40
Charlie James Russell (5) 40
Archie Miller (6) 41
Adanyah Connolly (7) 41
Evie Jones (7) 42
Issie Hubbard (6) 42
Alice Murrell (6) 43
Erin Starmer (6) 43
Rhys Owen (6) 44

Krishna Avanti Primary School, Leicester

Durgadevi Umakhanth (5) 44
Alekhya Nyasavajjala (5) 45
Manav Pandya (5) 45

Middleton Primary & Nursery School, Nottingham

Sophia Israr (6) 46
Maya Williams (7) 47
Harry James Hollings (6) 48
Fatimah Imaan Bhatti (6) 49
Molly Watson (6) 49
Zara Iqbal (6) 50
Uma Passi (6) 50
Adam Ditta (7) 51
Holly Gould (6) 51
Akash Sai Singh Virdi (7) 52
Agata Pasciak (7) 52
Ibrahim Shah (7) 53
Joseph Holmes (6) 53
Waail Iqbal (6) 54
George Sinski (6) 54
Leon Pearman (6) 55
Azahara Perez-Ball (6) 55
Rose Barrett (6) 56
Oliver Jakubiak 56
Zakariya Shah (7) 57

Moat Hall Primary School, Walsall

Taylor James Whittle (6) 57
Harry Stuart Bowles (7) 58
Sienna Brough (7) 58
Qiannah Malika Mills (6) 59
Phoebe Cooper (7) 59
Lexi Olivia Jarvis (6) 60
Cameron Howell (6) 60
Cameron Allen (6) 61
Roxylee Orme (6) 61
Olivia Peach (6) 62
Taylor-Mae Cooper 62
Summer Daisy Seymour (6) 63
Thomas James Hill (7) 63
Elliot Pearse (6) 64
Chloe Wheeldon (6) 64
Emily Mucklow (6) 65
Libby Tooker (6) 65
Elyse Jean Varley (7) 66
Drew Clarke (6) 66
Lucy Mai Stephenson (6) 67
Ella Ludgate (7) 67

Nonsuch Primary School, Birmingham

Gabriel Gordon (6) 68
Millie May Byrne (6) 68
Shiva Kochakorn Karimaghai (5) 69
Kayla Leigh Bird (6) 69
Keren Lusamba (6) 70
Amari Coleman (6) 70
Leshae Johnson (5) 71
Milly Milat Goitom (5) 71
Asia McLean (6) 72
Kara Morgan (6) 72

Pelsall Village School, Walsall

Leland Hartshorne (7) 73
Paige Helen Amelia Mason (7) 74
Megan Nicole Willetts (6) 74
Olivia Louise Boland (7) 75
Amber Porterfield (6) 75
Harvey Jack Showell (6) 76

Keira Mae Power (6) 76
Skye Swift (5) 77
Madison Duggan (7) 77
Elise-May Wood (7) 78
Summar Morag Linda Evans (6) 78
Abbie Ayles (6) 79
Riley Brookes (7) 79
Lexi-Mae Coney 80
George Bull (7) 80
Freya McGahan (5) 81
Madison Shinn (6) 81
Lacey Lou Taylor (7) 82
Ethan Williams 82
Aiden Reade (7) 83
Kian Mawby (7) 83
Bethlyn Rose Brotherton (6) 84
Owen Myles Hicken (6) 84
Harry G (6) 85
Lennon Ryan Hubbard (6) 85
Connor Alexander Duncan (6) 86
Brooke Olivia Westwood (6) 86
Jessica Wright (5) 87
Paul Joseph Lewis (6) 87
Sami Yusuf Demir (6) 88
Emily Billingham (7) 88
Kian Singh Sarai (5) 89
Libby-Anna Crook, Charley Green
& Kyle Lawrence (6) 89
William Swain (6) 90
Lilli-Mai Smith (5) 90
Kelsey Louise Follows (6) 91
Kian Maxwell (6) 91
Cole Dunn (7) 92
Caine-Jon Green (6) 92
Annabelle Whitelaw (7) 93
Alfie Lloyd (6) 93
Arlo Rigby (6) 94
Ruby H (5) 94
Doyle Paul Marson (6) 95
Daniel Shepherd (6) 95
Latoya Waterfield (6) 96
Grace L (6) 96
Jayden Waterfield (5) 97
April Charmaine Freeman (6) 97
Abigail Talbot (6) 97
Joel Humphries (6) 98
Addison Stokes (6) 98

Evie-Jane Dickinson (5)
& Holly R (6) 98

Robin Hood Primary School, Birmingham
Mohamed Ahmed (6) 99
Jannat Choudhury (6) 99
Musa Ahmed (6) 100
Zulekha Nasir (6) 100
Abdul Hadi (5) 101
Caitlyn Oliver (6) 101
Inaaya Nawaz (6) 102
Pragna Emani (6) 102
Morgan Simpson (6) 103
Willow Powell (6) 103
Summer Jones (6) 104
M Hamzah Qasim Alavi (6) 104
Alisha Ali (6) 105
Haniah Azad (6) 105
Aayah Rafique (6) 106
Kinza Ibrahmi (6) 106
Henry Howard (5) 107
Jerry Zhang (6) 107
Hanaa Ahmad (6) 108
Zymal Rehman (6) 108
Keira Brazier (6) 109
Hamza Rahman (6) 109
Pavan Chane (6) 110
Dante Nathaniel Pooler (6) 110
Laila Galloway (6) 111
Asher Phansi (6) 111
Sami Ahmad Anjam (6) 112
Umar Ahmed (6) 112
Sara Kayani (6) 112
Ibrahim Hussain (5) 113
Qiam Aariz Jamil (5) 113

St Christopher Primary School, Coventry
Lily Hamilton (5) 113
Chanel Marie Martin (5) 114
Rachel Butterworth (6) 114
Hannah Elizabeth Nicholls (5) 115
Eloise Heggie (6) 115
Reggie Jones (5) 116
Cohen Lily-Mae George (6) 116

Ebony Hanney (5) 117
Leyna Yeoman (5) 117
Carta Edward Galvin (6) 118
Poppy Eva Tegerdine (6) 118
Freya Davies (5) 119
Emma Hall 119

St Francis Xavier Catholic Primary School, Oldbury

Charlie Servando (6) 120
Harriet Moore (6) 120
Sorrel Hackett (7) 121
Amelie Hemmingway 121
Daniel Hurst 122
Macca Ros-Nalugon (6) 122
Izaak Ian Baillie (6) 123
Jacob Iezzi 123
Lacey Evans-Withers 124
Flynn Judge (6) 124
Alex Whitehouse 125
Anna 125
Lily Rose Marshall (6) 126
Kaja Roche 126
Ali 126

Stanion CE Primary School, Kettering

Rosa Hickinson (7) 127
Cobi Maddox (6) 127
Sasha Maita Badza (5) 128

Uppingham CE Primary School, Oakham

Cerys Neal (7) 128
Anna Williams (6) 129
Lexi Scott (6) 129
Lexi Foster (6) 130
Rian Nitesh Punja (5) 130
Katelyn Purdy (6) 131
Millie Rose Jasmine Tookey (6) 131
Alexia Grace Whitehead (6) 132

Maisie Draper (6) 132
Emily Hathaway (6) 133
Luke Billam (5) Deighton & Leah 133
Joseph Stacey (7) 134
Chloe Sheehan (5) 134
Riley Richardson (6) 135
Candy Zheng (6) 135
Olivia Benson (7) 136
Bella Banfield (5) 136
Charlie Burgess (6) 137
Scarlett Revitt (5) 137
Amelia Jolly (6) 138
Tia Nikia Pagan (5) 138
Grace Quirke (5) 139
Fletcher Dalby (5) 139
Evie Barnes (5) 140
Eden Lount (5) 140
Demi-Lee Lambert (4) 141
Joshua Burgess (4) 141
Maisie Richardson (4) 142
Imogen Grace Smith (5) 142
Brooke Nugent (4) 143
Thomas Williams (4) 143
Sofia Taylor (5) 144
Harrison Garrill (5) 144
Elise Foster (4) 145
Faith Young (4) 145
Noah Hopkinson (4) 146
Rosa Williams (4) 146
Eden Grace Isabella Tookey (4) 146
Zac Dumford-Finnemore (5) 147
Benjamin Williams (4) 147

Yew Tree Community School, Birmingham

Victor Joseph 147
Saarrah Begum (6) 148
Sahil Ahmed 148
Abdul Malik Mohammed 149
Subhaan Akram 149
Mohammed Mursalin (7) 150
Nabila Rizwan 150

THE POEMS

My First Acrostic – Poems From The Midlands

Ryan

R is for reading, I like reading books.
Y is for yellow. This is my favourite colour.
A is for active. I like playing and jumping.
N is for nice. I am always nice to people.

Ryan Patra (5)

Caitlin

C hatterbox
A lways kind
I am five
T wins brother and sister
L ove my mum and dad
I am beautiful
N ever stop dancing.

Caitlin Shirley Brown (5)
Ball Green Primary School, Stoke-On-Trent

Penguin

P enguins have webbed feet
E xcellent birds
N ot warm at night
G reat egg warming
U nder the sea
I n the night
N ice waters.

Tafira Enock Sambizi (6)
Ball Green Primary School, Stoke-On-Trent

Penguin

P redator
E gg warmer
N ever bad
G reat animal
U nbelievable animal
I n Antarctica
N ever sad.

Ruby Bourne (6)
Ball Green Primary School, Stoke-On-Trent

My First Acrostic – Poems From The Midlands

Penguin

P retty peckers
E gg warmers
N est builders
G orgeous
U nderwater
I ce swimmers
N ice birds.

Mackenzie Oxley (7)
Ball Green Primary School, Stoke-On-Trent

Penguin

P redator of fish
E gg layers
N ever warm
G ood divers
U nderwater
I n Antarctica
N ests for baby chicks.

Lillie-Mae McCue (7)
Ball Green Primary School, Stoke-On-Trent

Penguin

P enguins jump off cliffs
E ggs are warm
N est builders
G reat fish catchers
U nderwater animal
I n Antarctica
N ice webbed feet.

Jarome Moston (6)
Ball Green Primary School, Stoke-On-Trent

Penguin

P redator of fish
E mperor penguin
N est builder
G reat swimmers
U nder the water
I n Antarctica
N est warmer.

Lakelyn Jordan (7)
Ball Green Primary School, Stoke-On-Trent

Penguin

P redator
E gg warmer
N est builders
G o under water
U nderwater
I ncredible swimmers
N est.

Mitchell Sturgess (6)
Ball Green Primary School, Stoke-On-Trent

Penguin

P redator or swimmer
E gg warmers
N ot sunny
G ood at fishing
U nderwater
I n Antarctica
N ever warm.

Lucy Marie Phillips (7)
Ball Green Primary School, Stoke-On-Trent

Penguin

P redator of fish
E gg warmer
N est builder
G reat swimmers
U nderwater
I cy places
N on-flying bird.

Britton McKhai Leese (7)
Ball Green Primary School, Stoke-On-Trent

Penguin

P redator
E xcellent swimmers
N est builders
G reat fish catchers
U nbelievable
I n the night
N ever sad.

Elsie Kamili (7)
Ball Green Primary School, Stoke-On-Trent

Penguin

P redator swimmer
E gg warmer
N est maker
G lorious bird
U nderwater swimmers
I ncredible swimmers
N ever sad.

Millie Richards-Snape (7)
Ball Green Primary School, Stoke-On-Trent

Penguin

P redator of fish
E mperor bird
N ice black and white feathers
G lorious water divers
U nderwater divers
I cy Antarctica
N ice waddling.

Summer Lea (6)
Ball Green Primary School, Stoke-On-Trent

Penguin

P redator
E xcellent nest builders
N ever
G reat waddlers
U nbelievable
I ncredible
N ever sad.

Camron Ford (7)
Ball Green Primary School, Stoke-On-Trent

Penguin

P erfect birds
E xcellent flappers
N est builders
G lass sliders
U nderwater
I cy cold
N ice.

Ella Daley (7)
Ball Green Primary School, Stoke-On-Trent

My First Acrostic – Poems From The Midlands

Penguin

P enguins eat fish
E gg warmer
N est of rock
G ood swimmers
U nderwater
I cy land
N ever warm.

Antonia Meredith (6)
Ball Green Primary School, Stoke-On-Trent

Penguin

P ecking predators
E mperor penguins
N imble
G obble fish and krill
U nder the sea
I ncredible beaks
N ever fly.

Maxwell Mongo (7)
Ball Green Primary School, Stoke-On-Trent

Penguin

P redator pecker
E gg warmer
N est builder
G ood fishers
U nderwater swimmer
I ncredible diver
N ever sad.

Leah Key (6)
Ball Green Primary School, Stoke-On-Trent

Penguin

P retty
E gg
N ests
G ood
U nbelievable
I cy
N ice.

Tye Daniel Terry-Jones (6)
Ball Green Primary School, Stoke-On-Trent

Penguin

P enguins waddle
E xcellent swimmers
N ot warm
G obble fish
U nderwater
I cicles
N est builders.

Jaiden Richardson (7)
Ball Green Primary School, Stoke-On-Trent

Arctic

A bsolutely freezing
R ough sea
C ute polar bear
T iny penguin
I cicles are shiny
C old face.

Everlyn Catherine Peake (6)
Ball Green Primary School, Stoke-On-Trent

Arctic

A bsolutely freezing
R oaring polar bear
C old feet
T winkly snow
I gloo
C old snow.

Demi-Jo Bailey
Ball Green Primary School, Stoke-On-Trent

Arctic

A bsolutely freezing
R ough sea
C ute penguin and polar bear
T ickly polar bear
I cicles
C old penguin.

Chloe Kirk (6)
Ball Green Primary School, Stoke-On-Trent

Arctic

A ntarctica
R eally cold
C old snow
T winkly ice
I cy
C old toes.

Matthew Pritchard (5)
Ball Green Primary School, Stoke-On-Trent

Arctic

A ntarctica is his friend
R eally freezing
C old snow
T all penguins
I ce falls fast
C lever Eskimos.

Conner Robinson (6)
Ball Green Primary School, Stoke-On-Trent

Arctic

A bsolutely freezing
R ough wolves
C urious whales
T iny walruses
I gloos are not made of snow
C ute polar bears.

Brogan Michael Leese (6)
Ball Green Primary School, Stoke-On-Trent

Arctic

A ntarctica is his friend
R eally fat walrus
C old snow
T iny polar bear
I cicles hanging
C lever polar bear.

Dylan
Ball Green Primary School, Stoke-On-Trent

My First Acrostic – Poems From The Midlands

Arctic

A ntarctica
R eally freezing
C old toes
T winkly snow
I cy snow
C ute penguins.

Abi
Ball Green Primary School, Stoke-On-Trent

Arctic

A ntarctica
R eally cold
C old snow
T winkly snow
I t is white
C urious.

Louie Hughes
Ball Green Primary School, Stoke-On-Trent

Arctic

A bsolutely
R ough sea
C old cute
T iny penguin
I cicles
C urious Eskimo.

Matthew Russell Pritchard (5)
Ball Green Primary School, Stoke-On-Trent

Arctic

A ntarctica
R eally cold
C old polar bear
T winkly snow
I gloo
C old.

Bailee
Ball Green Primary School, Stoke-On-Trent

Arctic

A bsolutely freezing
R oaring polar bears
C old icicles
T oo cold fingers and hands
I ce is cold
C hilly cold ice.

Demi Bowers
Ball Green Primary School, Stoke-On-Trent

Arctic

A ll white and beautiful
R oaring polar bears
C old hands
T iny snowflakes
I cy igloo
C ute penguins.

Kaitlyn Skye Davies (6)
Ball Green Primary School, Stoke-On-Trent

Arctic

A ll white
R oaring polar bear
C old snow
T oo cold
I cy cold feet
C ute polar bear.

Maddie May Lucas (6)
Ball Green Primary School, Stoke-On-Trent

Keira

K eira is my name
E veryone is my friend
I am four
R eally beautiful eyes
A sister too.

Keira Upton
Ball Green Primary School, Stoke-On-Trent

Ella

E njoy dancing
L ovely and kind
L ittle but loud
A lways playing.

Ella Lyons
Ball Green Primary School, Stoke-On-Trent

Mikail Asim

'**M**y best friend is Danial,' he told me.
'**I** love my family,' I told my mum.
'**K**arate is a good sport,' said my dad.
'**A**m I good at football?' asked my dad.
'**I** am good at swimming,' said my dad
'**L**istening, are you good at that?' asked my mum.

'**I** am good at running,' said my dad.
'**I** am sleepy in the morning,' I told my dad.
I am going to the shop in the morning
'**M**y favourite game is PS4,' said my sister.

Mikail Asim Ahmed Siddiqui (7)
Brookside Primary School, Leicester

Untitled

L ollipops are tasty
I ce cream is cold
N uts are yucky
D oughnuts are delicious
A little girl.

S easons are great
P iles of leaves
R ain can fall to the ground
I cicles in winter full of delight
N o more snow tonight
G iant pieces of snow, how good.

F ins are good for fish
I ce cream they can't eat
S cenes make them happy
H appy, and happy.

H arry is my dad
O ranges are my favourite
R un all the way home
S pecial food just for you
E ggs are my favourite too.

B ananas are great
O ranges are tasty
B an them all

B ut the food you like
Y ellow is just like the sun.

S wim in the pool
U mbrellas twirling
M ahanimah is my friend
M eerab is my friend
E at quickly but don't exaggerate
R eally it is not true.

Linda Sun (6)
Brookside Primary School, Leicester

Miss Wells

M y best teacher
I like my class
S lippery Squares is my table
S chool is the best

W onderful teacher
E njoyable work
L ovely lady
L earning is fun
S inging numbers.

Emelia Bray (5)
Brookside Primary School, Leicester

Muhammad

M arvellous Muhammad
U nbelievably great
H as Lego
A nd racing cars
M errily plays
M onkey games
A nd
D inosaur bingo.

M uhammad
U ses
H is
A rm
M ovement to
M ime
A
D uck.

Muhammad Jagot (6)
Brookside Primary School, Leicester

Animals

B ees can sting people
E ach bee has two wings
E ggs are very small
S tinging bees have yellow and black stripes.

L ions eat meat
I nside the boundaries of a cage
O utrageous roar they have
N ew cubs stay with their mum.

M onkeys like bananas
O utside, swinging on vines
N apping on trees
K ick their legs out when they swing
E very monkey makes sounds
Y ou never know where you stand with monkey business.

Devan Kakkad (6)
Brookside Primary School, Leicester

Friends

F antastic
R eal fun
I will play
E ncourage you
N eed you
D oing fun together.

M y
I ce
S ugar
S weet

K ind
I ntelligent
N ice
G entle.

Arooj Rizwan Khatri (6)
Brookside Primary School, Leicester

My First Acrostic – Poems From The Midlands

Brookside

B rilliant – bright pupils
R is for respect – courteous children
O is for optimistic – positive in attitude
O is for outgoing – enthusiastic and daring
K is for kind – helpful to the society
S is for successful – achieve great heights
I is for inspired – motivated to do the best
D is for diligent – industrious and conscientious
E is for efficient – good in whatever they do.

Darsh Balasubramaniam (6)
Brookside Primary School, Leicester

Mohammed

M y mum is helpful
O melettes are yellow
H appy is my favourite song
A pples are red and juicy
M elons are green outside and red inside
M angoes are orange and very juicy
E ggs have a shell and break easily
D aggers are sharp, they hurt other people.

Mohammed-Hussain Patel (6)
Brookside Primary School, Leicester

Mustafa

M is for morals
U is for useful
S is for smart
T is for talented
A is for awesome
F is for friends
A is for active.

Mustafa Ahmed Lafta Alhindawe (5)
Brookside Primary School, Leicester

Rabbit

R abbits
A re
B eautiful
B ouncy and live
I nside
T heir burrows.

Sehrish Malik (5)
Brookside Primary School, Leicester

My First Acrostic – Poems From The Midlands

Layla

L ayla is excellent
A lways ready to help a person in need
Y ou will always have a friend in me
L ovely intelligent and kind
A pples are always my favourite food.

Layla Moonen-Patel (7)
Brookside Primary School, Leicester

Ikjot

I like ice cream
K is for kind
J is for jolly
O ranges are juicy
T rouble is my middle name.

Ikjot Kaur Sandhu (5)
Brookside Primary School, Leicester

Anum

A is for awesome
N is for naughty
U is for university
M is for I love my mummy.

Anum Hussain (7)
Brookside Primary School, Leicester

Miller Sweet

M iller is my name
I ce is cold which I can be
L ake is what I like to see
L azy is what I can be says mum
E xcellent that I try to be
R ough is how I play with my sister

S weet that I am
W illing is what I do best
E xcellent that I try
E ager to go to school
T rees are great.

Miller Sweet (5)
Granby Primary School, Leicester

My First Acrostic – Poems From The Midlands

Elephants

E xciting
L earners
E very day he travels with his mother
P laying, running, full of joy
H appy smiles
A slow walker
N o one can part this love
T hat elephant is fat
S haring.

Szymon Serwicki (7)
Granby Primary School, Leicester

Tia Burke

T is for teacher, I like to boss my dollies around.
I is for ink, I put pen to paper.
A is for alphabet, which I use to make words.
B is for beautiful, just like me.
U is for umbrella, what I take to school in the rain.
R is for running, I try to run as fast as the wind.
K is for kind, just like me.
E is for excited, I love to see my family.

Tia Grace Burke (6)
Granby Primary School, Leicester

Dinosaurs

D inichthys was the swimming one.
I guanodon was the speedy one.
N othosaurus was the fish-eating one.
O rnithocheirus was the walking and flying one.
S celidosaurus was the armoured one.
A llosaurus was the fierce one.
U tahraptor was the hunting one.
R hamphorynchus was the flying one.
S tegosaurus was the plant-eating one.

Jed Whittal-Williams (7)
Granby Primary School, Leicester

Penguins

P enguins eat juicy, fresh fish.
E ggs have little grey penguins in them.
N ice, cold, icy water just for them.
G rey, waddling babies dancing around.
U niform-type feathers to make them look smart.
I ncredible swimmers diving for fish.
N ever apart, always a family.
S earch for food to feed their babies.

Freya Kate Boniface (6)
Granby Primary School, Leicester

My First Acrostic – Poems From The Midlands

Tortoise

T ortoises are cute
O ur pet is a tortoise
R osie is her name
T hey live for many years, longer than us
O utdoors they like to explore
I ndoors they dig holes in the cage
S lowly they walk around
E very day we feed her things like lettuce.

Leah Halford-Jones (6)
Granby Primary School, Leicester

Jaydan

J aydan loves PlayStation, Minecraft best of all.
A mazing, awesome and funny and he is very tall.
Y ellow, blue and red are colours that he likes, but green is his favourite, it's the colour of his bike.
D rinking milk and munching toast.
A vengers, West Ham and Lego are what he loves most.
N o boring times, lots of fun, best brother, number one scn.

Jaydan James Whitmore (5)
Granby Primary School, Leicester

Arianit

A is for adorable because I am.
R is for ready, I am always ready for school.
I is for icicle, they hang off my roof.
A is for angel, my mum says I am.
N is for nanny, I love my nanny.
I is for instruments, I like music.
T is for teacher, I like my teacher.

Arianit Xhylani
Granby Primary School, Leicester

Joseph

J oker: He has a big gun!
O is for orange, that is you saying yum!
S is for snake, he hisses a lot!
E ating is a power, a lasso ties a knot!
P is for pea-brain. How much do you know?
H is for hump, climb up it so fast.

Joe Kiggell (6)
Granby Primary School, Leicester

Rabbit

R abbits like to play and sniff all day
A my's bunny sleeps on hay
B ernard's bunny breathes out ice
B ig bunnies catch mice
I don't like to see bunnies upset
T his class gives bunnies respect!

Saxon Nicholls (6)
Granby Primary School, Leicester

Rabbit

R abbits are cute
A pretty thing
B eautiful and fluffy
B rilliant bouncer
I n the fields, woodland and hutch is where they live
T eeth are big to munch their food.

Emmie Noon (6)
Granby Primary School, Leicester

Ananya

A is for awesome, that is what I am.
N is for nice, my friends say I am.
A is apple, I like apples.
N is for name, my name is Ananya.
Y is for yummy, ice cream is yummy.
A is for Aadya, that is my sister and she is my best friend.

Ananya Gulati (6)
Granby Primary School, Leicester

Rhino

R hinos are big
H ear them roar
I wonder if rhinoceroses snore
N ose horn is what rhino means
O n top of their heads you'll find these.

Maximillian Brown (7)
Granby Primary School, Leicester

Amber

A mber is my name
M ade in India and England
B am-Bam is my nickname
E ven my sister says so
R ed hot temper that's me.

Amber Kaur Supria (6)
Granby Primary School, Leicester

Tiger

T igers are kings of the jungle
I ncredibly scary when he gets angry
G rowls, especially when he gets hungry.
E ndangered species in India.
R unning, looking for their prey.

Krish Sookye (7)
Granby Primary School, Leicester

Alfie

A is for amazing
L is for loving
F is for friendly
I is for intelligent
E is for excellent.

Alfie Snow (5)
Granby Primary School, Leicester

Josh

J is for joker, I love playing tricks on my daddy.
O is for outgoing, I love joining in.
S is for sporty, I love watching and playing football.
H is for happy, I always am.

Joshua Marvell
Granby Primary School, Leicester

Theo

T is for talented because I can do front flips.
H is for hungry, I have a hungry tummy.
E is for exercise because I like swimming.
O is for oranges because I like making juice.

Theo Dixon (6)
Granby Primary School, Leicester

Lexi

L is for lovely little girl.
E is for enjoying swimming.
X is for my exciting dance moves.
I is for independent which I always try to be.

Lexi Smales (5)
Granby Primary School, Leicester

Mia

M is for monkey, I am very cheeky
I is for ice cream, it is my favourite pudding
A is for Ananya and Amber, they are my best friends.

Mia Bayle-Kuhn (6)
Granby Primary School, Leicester

Snow Leopard

S neaky creatures
N ot always kind
O ut in the snow
W orking a lot in the day

L oving and kind
E ats meat
O nly white
P awing in the snow.
A lways covered in snow.
R uns really fast.
D usty nose covered.

Megan Connie Brightman (7)
Greens Norton CE Primary School, Towcester

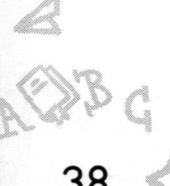

My First Acrostic – Poems From The Midlands

Samuel

S is for Samuel, I am very kind.
A is for amazingly clever.
M is for mighty and strong.
U is for using 100 squares.
E is for everyone's friend.
L is for laughing every day.

Samuel Miller (5)
Greens Norton CE Primary School, Towcester

Thompson

T alking a lot
H elpful
O ften kind
M um to children
P ouncing around
S ometimes cool
O ften fancy
N ot bad.

Charlie Bottomley (7)
Greens Norton CE Primary School, Towcester

Dolphin

D ives in the water
O ften helpful
L ovely and kind
P layful all the time
H ere they dive
I n the swimming pool they swim
N ot naughty.

Andrew Doig (6)
Greens Norton CE Primary School, Towcester

Octopus

O ctopus has three brains
C atching fish to eat and little creatures
T he octopus is very big
O ctopus has eight tentacles
P redators come and eat the octopus
U nder the water the octopus lives under the rocks
S harks eat the octopus.

Charlie James Russell (5)
Greens Norton CE Primary School, Towcester

Unicorn

U sing a horn to protect himself.
N ot always running only if it's under attack.
I t's a big, kind magical horse.
C reature's beautiful tail.
O n the beautiful side and dark side.
R iding it.
N oisy animal.

Archie Miller (6)
Greens Norton CE Primary School, Towcester

Adanyah

A lways kind
D oing the right stuff
A lways helpful
N ot mean
Y elling like a cockerel
A terrific girl
H elping others.

Adanyah Connolly (7)
Greens Norton CE Primary School, Towcester

Dolphin

D ives into water
O ften nice and kind
L ovely to listen to
P lays all day
H ides when you scare them
I n the glittery water
N ever naughty.

Evie Jones (7)
Greens Norton CE Primary School, Towcester

Horse

H er rider rides it
O ne of my favourite animals
R ides on the fields
S ome eat grass
E ats hay.

Issie Hubbard (6)
Greens Norton CE Primary School, Towcester

Alice

A is for apples, I like apples.
L is for Lego Friends, I like to build things.
I is for inside, I like to be inside my house.
C is for candy canes, candy canes are the best.
E is for everyone can be my friend.

Alice Murrell (6)
Greens Norton CE Primary School, Towcester

Tiger

T errible kindness
I t's often hunting
G ets warm in the summer
E ver so scary
R eady to hunt in the night.

Erin Starmer (6)
Greens Norton CE Primary School, Towcester

Panda

P adding around.
A dding babies.
N aughty.
D irty paws.
A ll around the forest.

Rhys Owen (6)
Greens Norton CE Primary School, Towcester

Autumn

A ll of the cute squirrels dig up acorns.
U mbrellas keep you dry from the wet leaves.
T iny red berries come out.
U nderground animals hibernate.
M uddy, yucky, muddy ground.
N uts fall.

Durgadevi Umakhanth (5)
Krishna Avanti Primary School, Leicester

Autumn

A ll brown nuts fall off the trees.
U mbrellas to keep you dry.
T he leaves get crunchy when you stamp.
U nder the trees there are crunchy leaves.
M uddy puddles on the ground.
N uts fall off trees.

Alekhya Nyasavajjala (5)
Krishna Avanti Primary School, Leicester

Spring

S pring is fun
P erfect day
R oses grow
I t is a lovely day
N ow days get long
G o to the park.

Manav Pandya (5)
Krishna Avanti Primary School, Leicester

Transport

T rains go really fast through tunnels.
R ockets shooting into space.
A eroplanes flying through the clouds.
N eil Armstrong was the first person to fly a rocket to the moon.
S hips sailing slowly on the sea.
P eople in cars driving fast.
O range rocket zooming into space.
R acing cars going extremely fast.
T rams chugging quickly on the winding tracks.

Sophia Israr (6)
Middleton Primary & Nursery School, Nottingham

My First Acrostic – Poems From The Midlands

Transport

T rains run through the meadows like a tornado in the screaming wind.
R acing car making its way to the finish line.
A eroplanes zooming through the air, 'To Australia finally,' said Amy Johnson.
N uts get tangled in Lewis Hamilton's racing car engine. 'Oh no!' panicked Lewis.
S hips sail the seas in stormy weather.
P eople cheering for Amy Johnson when she returned to London.
O ctopuses attacking the ships in bright sunrise.
R un down to get to the finish line of the racing track, quick before you lose!
T rams by horse – not anymore, that was the past.

Maya Williams (7)
Middleton Primary & Nursery School, Nottingham

Transport

T all cruisers sailing towards faraway lands, it gets noisier when it sails through the rattling, rumbling sea.
R ockets steaming ahead of people. They like to zoom to the moon with people inside of them.
A cross the track trains go *clickety-clack* going to cities, starting at Nottingham and travelling to Manchester.
N eil Armstrong wanted to get to the moon first and step on the moon.
S ome vehicles zoom past you when you are running to beat them.
P oems are being shared to other people even right now, they like to share with their brothers.
O riginal cars across the land are powered by fuel.
R ockets zooming to lots of planets in our solar system.
T raffic jams with our cars that humans invented.

Harry James Hollings (6)
Middleton Primary & Nursery School, Nottingham

My First Acrostic – Poems From The Midlands

Transport

T rams going *clickety-clack!*
R ockets zooming into space.
A eroplanes whooshing through the air.
N eil Armstrong zooming to the moon.
S hips sailing across the sea and there's lightning in the sky.
P eople can ride on any transport
O n your scooter or riding a bike is really fun, am I right?
R ockets going very fast.
T rains whooshing past on the train tracks.

Fatimah Imaan Bhatti (6)
Middleton Primary & Nursery School, Nottingham

Cars And Boats

C ars go fast on the road
A car goes speedy fast
R acing cars go zooming
S ome cars to 90 miles an hour.

B oats go fast like motorboats
O n boats they take people across the stormy seas
A boat can be a speed boat or a normal boat
T ravelling boats going across the sunny seas.

Molly Watson (6)
Middleton Primary & Nursery School, Nottingham

Transport

T rains chugging about on the track
R oaring motorbikes zooming across the streets
A Lamborghini whooshing down the road
N eil Armstrong was the first man to walk on the moon
S pongy cars cannot be made
P ebbles, big and small, all over the road
O ld classic cars are driven around slowly
R acing rockets zooming to the moon
T rams racing quickly on their track.

Zara Iqbal (6)
Middleton Primary & Nursery School, Nottingham

Boats

B oats are really speedy.
O n a boat you can get to a different country.
A boat is big and shiny.
T rillions of boats are really really shiny.
S ails on the ships out at sea.

Uma Passi (6)
Middleton Primary & Nursery School, Nottingham

Transport

T rains going on the rackety tracks
R acing cars going fast
A eroplanes are very long
N eil Armstrong was the first person to walk on the moon.
S ports cars are extremely fast.
P ower makes trains go fast on their tracks.
O range flames coming out of the rocket.
R acing cars go extremely fast
T rains zoom through the rockety tracks.

Adam Ditta (7)
Middleton Primary & Nursery School, Nottingham

Train

T rains have two sides to drive on
R unning along the tracks
A train goes extremely fast in town
I n a city you can see trains.
N othing is faster than a train.

Holly Gould (6)
Middleton Primary & Nursery School, Nottingham

Transport

T rains darting through the terrifying tunnel.
R ails are shiny, dashing on the ground.
A submarine under the sparkling sea.
N ine cars zooming down the horrible hill.
S even colourful aeroplanes travelling in the grizzly night.
P rancing boat in the sparkling night.
O ver-roaring car on the rough road.
R ough boat in the sparkly sea.
T rains terrifyingly blasting down the metal railway.

Akash Sai Singh Virdi (7)
Middleton Primary & Nursery School, Nottingham

Train

T rains ride on tracks
R ocket was the fastest train
A train can get very fast
I nside the train are passengers
N oisy trains speeding by.

Agata Pasciak (7)
Middleton Primary & Nursery School, Nottingham

Transport

T rams go very fast in 2015.
R acing cars are fast.
A eroplanes are very long.
N eil Armstrong is the first to go to the moon.
S hips sailing on the sea.
P ower makes trains go fast on the track.
O range ships sailing in a dark, stormy sea.
R acing cars zooming through the track.
T rains go zooming through the tracks.

Ibrahim Shah (7)
Middleton Primary & Nursery School, Nottingham

Train

T rains darting on the rickety tracks,
R ails rusty along the rattling planks of wood,
A nother train is coming,
I saw a train, it was whooshing,
N o more red trains are coming.

Joseph Holmes (6)
Middleton Primary & Nursery School, Nottingham

Transport

T rains go on very, very long tracks.
R acing cars go fast on racing tracks.
A eroplanes flying through foggy clouds.
N eil Armstrong was the first man to step on the moon.
S hips sail on stormy dark seas.
P lanes are zooming through white clouds.
O range ships sail through stormy seas.
R ockets fly through space to the moon.
T rains go very deep into tunnels.

Waail Iqbal (6)
Middleton Primary & Nursery School, Nottingham

Ship

S parkly ship zooming through the massive waves
H uge ship bouncing on the bronze waves
I nside the shiny deck
P owering the colourful and zooming ship with sparkly petrol.

George Sinski (6)
Middleton Primary & Nursery School, Nottingham

Transport

T rains are zooming
R ails are flat
A boat is blasting on the sea
N ine vans are zooming
S peed boats are zooming in the sea
P lanes are diving through the sky
O ne blasting motorbike is going
R oaring boats zooming in the sea
T rams whoosh on the track.

Leon Pearman (6)
Middleton Primary & Nursery School, Nottingham

Boat

B eeping shiny high horns.
O pening the shimmery doors.
A white boat zooming on the sparkly, bumpy sea.
T he beautiful, twinkly oceans.

Azahara Perez-Ball (6)
Middleton Primary & Nursery School, Nottingham

Transport

T rains are very fast and very speedy.
R acing cars are speedy.
A train goes clickety-clack on the track.
N eil Armstrong was the first man on the moon
S pace rockets can carry you to space in a flash.
P eople can travel on every type of transport.
O range flames shooting out of the colourful rocket.
R acing cars are very speedy to go to the finish line.
T rains can be all different kinds of speeds.

Rose Barrett (6)
Middleton Primary & Nursery School, Nottingham

Boat

B lasting across the red surface
O ozilly going across the shiny sea
A lways floating across the watery waves
T racking lots of rough waves.

Oliver Jakubiak
Middleton Primary & Nursery School, Nottingham

Cars

C ars can go super speedy
A car can drive up to one whole hour
R acing cars are the fastest cars in the whole world
S ometimes fast cars go at the speed of lightning.

Zakariya Shah (6)
Middleton Primary & Nursery School, Nottingham

Taylor Whittle

T rains are my favourite thing
A eroplanes are helpful because you can go on holiday
Y oghurt I like
L ego I like
O ut, I like going out
R abbits, I like rabbits

W ood is helpful
H orses are furry
I nformation is very helpful
T rolleys are very helpful
T rucks are very helpful
L ollipops I love
E lectricity is very helpful.

Taylor James Whittle (6)
Moat Hall Primary School, Walsall

Harry Bowles

H amsters are my favourite pets
A merica is the best holiday
R abbits are my favourite animals
R acing is the best
Y ear Two is the best

B ananas, I hate them so much
O ranges are the best fruit
W alking is exhausting to me
L ollipops are lovely to me
E mily is the best sister ever
S ea Life Centres are hot for me.

Harry Stuart Bowles (7)
Moat Hall Primary School, Walsall

Sienna

S chool is great, sandwiches are yummy and scrumptious
I nvitations are exciting
E nvelopes you can use for cards
N ew, it is new
N ame is a name
A bove is up in the sky.

Sienna Brough (7)
Moat Hall Primary School, Walsall

Qiannah Mills

Q ueen Elizabeth is my favourite
I nsect bit me
A crobats are what is love
N ever stop drinking that's what I do
A ll About That Bass is my favourite song
H ave some chocolate every day

M iss Stott is my favourite teacher in the world
I ce is cold on me
L ollipops are my favourite
L ovely days
S hopping is my favourite thing to do.

Qiannah Malika Mills (6)
Moat Hall Primary School, Walsall

Phoebe

P enguins are my favourite bird
H elpful people are my friends
O n my shelves everything is organised
E xcited people are my favourite
B allerina dolls are cute
E lephants are my favourite big animal.

Phoebe Cooper (7)
Moat Hall Primary School, Walsall

Lexi Jarvis

L ovely dresses I have
E mma is my friend's mum
X -ray is not my favourite thing
I ce cream is my favourite treat
J okes make my family laugh
A ll About That Bass by Megan Trainer is my favourite song
R omantic shoes I have
V iolet is a flower
I ngrid is my favourite name
S illy people I don't like.

Lexi Olivia Jarvis (6)
Moat Hall Primary School, Walsall

Cameron

C amouflaging is my favourite thing to do
A thletics is my favourite sport
M otorbikes are my favourite vehicle
E nemies are my favourite opponents
R adios I listen to
O pponents are my rivals
N etball is sometimes my favourite.

Cameron Howell (6)
Moat Hall Primary School, Walsall

Cameron

C ake is my favourite
A pples are good for me
M y favourite tea is pasta
E lephants are big
R ainbows are colourful
O pening the toys
N oses can be itchy.

Cameron Allen (6)
Moat Hall Primary School, Walsall

Roxylee

R oxylee feels happy
O rme – obstinate
X -ray – noun
Y ou – pronoun
L ove I like
E xcellent
E ggs.

Roxylee Orme (6)
Moat Hall Primary School, Walsall

Olivia

O ctopi are nice
L ook at me, I am dancing
I nsects are scary
V ans are big
I ce cream is yummy
A pples are crunchy.

Olivia Peach (6)
Moat Hall Primary School, Walsall

Taylor

T igers are my favourite
A crobatics
Y o-yos are fun
L ollies are yummy
O h it is cold
R iding my bike is fun.

Taylor-Mae Cooper
Moat Hall Primary School, Walsall

My First Acrostic – Poems From The Midlands

Summer

S inging is what I like to do best
U mbrella is what I use when it rains
M oney buys me nice stuff
M onkeys make me laugh so much
E lephants are really tall
R abbits are super small.

Summer Daisy Seymour (6)
Moat Hall Primary School, Walsall

Thomas

T ea is my favourite drink
H amburger is my favourite food
O ne time a bird pooed on me
M um says when I get home, 'Go and get your pyjamas on.'
A djectives I am really good at
S ometimes I am silly.

Thomas James Hill (7)
Moat Hall Primary School, Walsall

Elliot

E njoy playing football
L ike sports
L ove my motorbike
I like Year Two
O n Tuesday I do guitar lessons
T elevision is very good.

Elliot Pearse (6)
Moat Hall Primary School, Walsall

Chloe

C akes, chocolate and caramel are my favourite things to eat
H elpful people are my best friends
L ovely, long hair
O rganised and tidy
E xcited and helpful.

Chloe Wheeldon (6)
Moat Hall Primary School, Walsall

Emily

E at my food that is delicious
M y mom is special
I have an idea, we all work together
L ift things to move them
Y oung forever!

Emily Mucklow (6)
Moat Hall Primary School, Walsall

Libby

L ittle I am
I ce cream is nice
B rothers are annoying
B ubbles are white
Y o-yos are fun to play with.

Libby Tooker (6)
Moat Hall Primary School, Walsall

Elyse

E lsa likes experiments and everyone
L ike the lab and the library
Y ellow yo-yo looks lovely
S ad and crying
E lephants love to eat.

Elyse Jean Varley (7)
Moat Hall Primary School, Walsall

Drew

D rawing is my favourite thing
R obots are my favourite
E gg on toast is my favourite
W inter is my favourite season.

Drew Clarke (6)
Moat Hall Primary School, Walsall

Lucy

L eeks are my favourite food
U nicorn is my favourite toy
C amels are my favourite animal
Y ellow is my favourite colour.

Lucy Mai Stephenson (6)
Moat Hall Primary School, Walsall

Ella

E lephants are my favourite animal
L aying the table is my favourite
L eigha is my cousin
A rt is my favourite.

Ella Ludgate (7)
Moat Hall Primary School, Walsall

Dog

D ogs like sniffing
O nly small dogs can hide
G igantic dogs can run fast.

Gabriel Gordon (6)
Nonsuch Primary School, Birmingham

Rabbit

R abbits eats carrots
A rabbit hops around
B ig rabbits have furry coats
B ouncy rabbits have pink ears
I like small rabbits
T iny rabbits hide away.

Millie May Byrne (6)
Nonsuch Primary School, Birmingham

My First Acrostic – Poems From The Midlands

Rabbit

R abbits like to play
A rabbit hops
B rown rabbits are different
B ut they like jumping
I s a rabbit bouncy or not?
T ired rabbits are different.

Shiva Kochakorn Karimaghai (5)
Nonsuch Primary School, Birmingham

Rabbit

R abbits eat carrots
A rabbit has lots of fur
B ut rabbits hop a lot
B ut they are really fluffy
I think rabbits are adorable
T he rabbit lives in a hole.

Kayla Leigh Bird (6)
Nonsuch Primary School, Birmingham

Rabbit

R abbits are fluffy
A rabbit is a bunny
B rown rabbits are different
B unnies are pink and white
I nside they play
T ake too long outside.

Keren Lusamba (6)
Nonsuch Primary School, Birmingham

Monkey

M onkeys jump
O n the trees
N ow monkey stands on the bar
K eep swinging like a monkey
E at bananas
Y oung monkeys are small.

Amari Coleman (6)
Nonsuch Primary School, Birmingham

My First Acrostic – Poems From The Midlands

Rabbit

R abbits like to jump
A cross the river
B ut they fall in
B lack and white
I like rabbits
T he rabbit likes to play.

Leshae Johnson (5)
Nonsuch Primary School, Birmingham

Rabbit

R abbits live in a hole
A rabbit is a furry animal
B unny rabbit jumps all around
B oing, boing, boing!
I t is sleeping
T eeth are sharp.

Milly Milat Goitom (5)
Nonsuch Primary School, Birmingham

Bunny

B unny rabbits jump up and down
U nder the bed it hides
N ighttime it sleeps in a hutch
N ow it is eating carrots
Y ou are lovely and soft.

Asia McLean (6)
Nonsuch Primary School, Birmingham

Robin

R obins can fly
O wls and robins are friends
B ig wings on a robin
I like small robins
N ice robins fly with each other.

Kara Morgan (6)
Nonsuch Primary School, Birmingham

Antarctica

A ntarctica is colder than the North Pole because it is right, right down south
N obody lives there at all because there is no heat
T all, huge icebergs float across the transparent water
A ntarctica is the coldest place on Earth
R unning across the ice before it melts or cracks
C old is everywhere in sight
T all igloos can be built there and people shelter themselves
I t is so cold that some people
C annot live there
A ntarctica is colder than the North Pole.

Leland Hartshorne (7)
Pelsall Village School, Walsall

Antarctic

A t Antarctica the snow is as cold as a chilly freezer
N othing is warm in Antarctica because it is not near the equator
T ravelling across the slippery ice is dangerous
A nimals hibernate in Antarctica because it is cold
R anging icebergs float across the sea while the snow storm goes on
C rashing storms make the poor penguins chilly
T emperature in Antarctica is -79 degrees
I n Antarctica frostbiting wind blows quickly
C onfusing.

Paige Helen Amelia Mason (7)
Pelsall Village School, Walsall

Winter

W hy is it chilly winter?
I n winter why do we wear hats?
N ear there are snow dogs in winter
T he snowman is chilly and cold
E veryone is crackling tiny, sparkling, twinkling snowflakes
R eflective snowflakes twinkle in the dark.

Megan Nicole Willetts (6)
Pelsall Village School, Walsall

My First Acrostic – Poems From The Midlands

Antarctic

A nimals live in Antarctica
N o huskies are allowed in Antarctica
T all icebergs float across the cold sea
A fur seal lives in Antarctica
R aging winds blow across the ice
C ars don't drive in Antarctica because people don't live in Antarctica
T emperature drops way down low
I n Antarctica emperor penguins live
C old winds blow in Antarctica.

Olivia Louise Boland (7)
Pelsall Village School, Walsall

Winter

W indy, swirling snowflakes fly faster than a car in the snow storm
I ce is slippy and can break into icebergs
N o leaves are on the trees in winter
T he cold air hits your freezing face and makes it tingle
E veryone must wear a warm, snug coat
R ain is slushy when mixed with snow on the roads.

Amber Porterfield (6)
Pelsall Village School, Walsall

Snowflake

S now falls from the blue sky
N obody wants to go inside
O utside the snow is flying
W hite snow falls from the blue sky
F rozen land
L ots of children having fun
A very happy day
K eep on snowing
E veryone is in bed.

Harvey Jack Showell (6)
Pelsall Village School, Walsall

Winter

W hen the sun sets it looks a sparkly diamond shape
I ce is cold as an icicle
N ear Antarctica there are a lot of penguins and it is hard for them to find each other
T he icebergs can be all different sizes
E arly, when the penguins have to go right to the end of Antarctica it takes about 8 weeks –
R eally! The dads wave goodbye.

Keira Mae Power (6)
Pelsall Village School, Walsall

Snowflake

S nowflakes fall from the sky
N orth Pole is cold
O h, blow the snow
W e go outside
F rozen lands
L ittle, cold hands
A ll blow the snowflakes
K eep ourselves warm
E veryone is smiling.

Skye Swift (5)
Pelsall Village School, Walsall

Winter

W hite snow is falling gently through the icy air
I mpressive snowflakes are falling carefully on the snowy ground
N ot hot in winter, because it is frozen in winter
T he snow is freezing because it is winter
E veryone had fun in winter
R ain is dropping because it is a wet, soggy, rainy day.

Madison Duggan (7)
Pelsall Village School, Walsall

Antarctic

A ntarctica has penguins that chatter
N ever warm in winter because of snow
T here are no people living in Antarctica
A s time went on there were no husky dogs allowed
R idged icebergs are freezing because they're in a cold place
C old in Antarctic places
T here are little snow-houses travelling towards the ground
I n Antarctica there are no white, fluffy polar bears
C old icicles in snowy winter!

Elise-May Wood (7)
Pelsall Village School, Walsall

Winter

W hy is it so windy and cold in winter?
I like making snowmen in winter in the cold and melting snow
N othing gets warm in winter, it is the cold season
T he cold snow is crying out
E ven though it is cold in winter it is also windy
R ough, cold snow is crying out because it is rough.

Summar Morag Linda Evans (6)
Pelsall Village School, Walsall

Snowflake

S oft like a pillow
N owhere to be seen, animals hide away
O utside the streets turn white
W indy snow flies towards my face
F luffy, like a puppy
L ovely, like flowers
A ll around the snowflakes twirl
K ick the snow like leaves
E verywhere the ground is all snow.

Abbie Ayles (6)
Pelsall Village School, Walsall

Winter

W hy is ice so smooth?
I n winter it's the coldest place on Earth
N o people lived in Antarctica, only insects
T ransparent rain is very cold in winter
E veryone doesn't like winter, but some people do
R ain is transparent.

Riley Brookes (7)
Pelsall Village School, Walsall

Antarctia

A ntarctica is freezing cold
N ot one person has gone there, because nobody likes snow
T wo scientists went there once
A nimals that live there have got fur
R ain falls down quickly and fast
C old in Antarctica because there is snow there
T here are tall, snowy mountains because there
I s bad weather
C old is all around at the South Pole.

Lexi-Mae Coney
Pelsall Village School, Walsall

Winter

W inter is frosty
I n the winter it is cold and freezing
N o sun in winter
T he ice is frozen
E veryone plays in winter
R ain is transparent.

George Bull (7)
Pelsall Village School, Walsall

Snowflake

S nowflakes fall from the sky
N orth Pole is cold
O h, blow the snow
W e go outside
F alling snowflakes
L ittle, cold hands
A ll day we play with the snowflakes
K eep warm
E nd of the day we go to bed.

Freya McGahan (5)
Pelsall Village School, Walsall

Winter

W hy does it snow in winter?
I cicles are really spiky and cold
N o one likes frost because it is cold
T he snow can melt in the bright sun
E veryone needs warm clothes
R aindrops can fall down.

Madison Shinn (6)
Pelsall Village School, Walsall

Antarctic

A ntarctica is as cold as crunchy ice
N o people live in Antarctica
T he penguins carry their eggs in their feet
A ntarctica has a lot of penguins
R ain comes down a lot in Antarctica
C old is all around the animals' habitats
T he polar bears are as fluffy as a blanket
I n Antarctica it is really, really cold
C ould it be really hot, like summer in Antarctica?

Lacey Lou Taylor (7)
Pelsall Village School, Walsall

Frost

F rost is very cold
R ed, chilly noses on children
O n the ground is icy ice
S ometimes frost can be cold
T he frost is super-duper cold.

Ethan Williams
Pelsall Village School, Walsall

My First Acrostic – Poems From The Midlands

Antarctic

A ntarctic is the coldest place
N o people live in this cold place
T all penguins slide on their bellies to get in
A nimals are really good in the cold
R eally cold wind blows
C rashing is really bad
T emperature in Antarctic is really cold
I n Antarctic people don't live near
C old icebergs are big because it can break ice.

Aiden Reade (7)
Pelsall Village School, Walsall

Frost

F rost is so cold in winter, we do get a lot of snow
R ain is so watery because rain comes out as shiny bright
O xygen is air, it gives you more power
S now can freeze if you are in a blizzard
T ransparent, you can see through tiny snowflakes.

Kian Mawby (7)
Pelsall Village School, Walsall

Snowflake

S oft like a polar bear's fur
N ice as a diamond
O utside the streets were white
W hite as snow
F luffy like the clouds
L ittle snowflakes falling
A ll the ground was covered in white snow
K icking the nice, soft snow
E verywhere is white.

Bethlyn Rose Brotherton (6)
Pelsall Village School, Walsall

Frost

F rosty icicles are as sharp as crackers
R ain can fall, but it can't snow all the time
O wls freeze across the frosty night
S nowmen are made with white, soft snow
T he temperature is very cold in Antarctica.

Owen Myles Hicken (6)
Pelsall Village School, Walsall

Snowflake

S oft and cosy like a huge white blanket
N ow the snow falls even faster
O utside the streets turn white
W atching the snow fall down from the sky
F lakes as white as ice cream
L ittle snowflakes
A ll the children went outside to make a snowman
K ick the snow with your feet
E veryone loves snow.

Harry G (6)
Pelsall Village School, Walsall

Frost

F rozen ice covers the cold fields
R aindrops fall from the heavenly sky
O ther people throw snowballs when it snows
S nowballs are freezing cold
T ransparent rain falls onto the cold concrete.

Lennon Ryan Hubbard (6)
Pelsall Village School, Walsall

Snowflake

S oft and cosy like a snuggly white blanket
N ighttime come and the snow still falls
O utside is all white
W onderful white snow
F alls like beautiful angels
L ovely and soft like fur
A ll the children go out to play
K icking the snow on the ground
E veryone likes snow.

Connor Alexander Duncan (6)
Pelsall Village School, Walsall

Frost

F urry animals hibernate in winter
R aindrops are not good
O n winter days it is chilly
S nowflakes twist and twirl through the wind
T he frost is glittering white, sparkly and shiny.

Brooke Olivia Westwood (6)
Pelsall Village School, Walsall

Snowflake

S nowflakes falling from the sky
N o one likes to stay inside
O utside everyone is excited
W onderland is fun
F un, fun, fun! Children build a snowman
L aughing people having fun
A mazed children are outside
K eep on having fun
E veryone is having fun outside.

Jessica Wright (5)
Pelsall Village School, Walsall

Frost

F rosty snowflakes fall at Christmas
R usty grass turns crunchy
O wls freeze at night
S nowballs are used as weapons
T ransparent rain falls into cold.

Paul Joseph Lewis (6)
Pelsall Village School, Walsall

Snowflake

S nowflakes floating from the sky
N o one likes to stay inside
O utside it is cold
W onderful and it's fun
F un, fun fun!
L ots of children went to bed
A mazed children outside
K eep happy
E veryone is having fun outside.

Sami Yusuf Demir (6)
Pelsall Village School, Walsall

Frost

F rost is frozen
R ocks with frost
O ver the rocks there's some trees covered in frost
S now is falling on top of the frost
T he frost is sparkling.

Emily Billingham (7)
Pelsall Village School, Walsall

Snowflake

S now falls from the blue skies
N o one likes to stay inside
O utside is cold
W onderland is fun
F un! Children build a snowman
L aughing people having fun
A happy snowman that can't move
K eep on having fun
E verybody is having fun in the snow.

Kian Singh Sarai (5)
Pelsall Village School, Walsall

Ice

I cy, sparkling and shining like diamonds
C runching like crisps under our feet
E asy to crack and shatter like glass.

**Libby-Anna Crook, Charley Green
& Kyle Lawrence (6)**
Pelsall Village School, Walsall

Snowflake

S nowflakes falling from the sky
N orth Pole
O utside it is cold
W onderful fun
F un, fun fun!
L ots of children outside
A mazed children outside
K eep ourselves warm
E xcited people everywhere.

William Swain (6)
Pelsall Village School, Walsall

Snow

S now is crunchy
N ice to play in the snow
O utside the snow shines like the sun
W onderful snow falls from the sky.

Lilli-Mai Smith (5)
Pelsall Village School, Walsall

Snowflake

S nowflakes falling from the sky
N orth Pole
O utside there is lots of snow
W onderland is fun
F un! Children build a snowman
L ater on the children went to bed
A mazed children outside
K eep warm
E veryone is having fun outside.

Kelsey Louise Follows (6)
Pelsall Village School, Walsall

Snow

S parkly as a diamond
N ice as a polar bear
O utside children build a snowman
W onderful snow lays on the ground.

Kian Maxwell (6)
Pelsall Village School, Walsall

Antarctic

A ntarctica is very cold
N o husky dogs!
T all, sharp icebergs
A lot of waddling penguins!
R aging, cold wind
C old ice blocks
T all, sharp icebergs
I want to come here!
C old ice blocks.

Cole Dunn (7)
Pelsall Village School, Walsall

Snow

S now is cold
N ot very warm
O utside the snow is sinking
W et look world.

Caine-Jon Green (6)
Pelsall Village School, Walsall

My First Acrostic – Poems From The Midlands

Antarctic

A ntarctic is a chilly place with lots of ice like cold water
N ow polar bears are allowed to go in the Antarctic
T all, vast mountains can be in the Antarctic as well
A ll penguins and seals live in the Antarctic
R ippling water melts down the cold icicles
C old winds blow in the Antarctic
T all, sharp icebergs hang
I ce is really cold in the Antarctic
C old seals and penguins live in the Antarctic.

Annabelle Whitelaw (7)
Pelsall Village School, Walsall

Snow

S now falls from the sky
N obody wants to go inside
O utside it is cold
W hite, snowy day.

Alfie Lloyd (6)
Pelsall Village School, Walsall

Snowflake

S nowflakes fall down in the distance
N orth Pole
O utside it is cold
W hen it is snowing the children go out
F un, fun, fun!
L ots of children outside
A mazing children collecting
K eep ourselves warm
E xcited people.

Arlo Rigby (6)
Pelsall Village School, Walsall

Snow

S oft and cold like ice
N ice and fluffy like a cloud
O utside the snow is crunchy like crisps
W hirling and twirling from the sky.

Ruby H (5)
Pelsall Village School, Walsall

Snowflake

S nowflakes falling
N orth Pole
O utside it is cold
W onderful fun
F un children
L aughter everywhere
A ir around is frosty
K eep warm
E xcellent fun.

Doyle Paul Marson (6)
Pelsall Village School, Walsall

Snow

S oft and cold like ice
N ice and fluffy
O utside the snow is crunchy like crisps
W hirling and twirling from the sky.

Daniel Shepherd (6)
Pelsall Village School, Walsall

Antarctic

A ntarctica has lots of penguins
N o polar bears in Antarctica
T he jellyfish live in the sea
A nd the snow falls and twirls through the wind
R idged snow storms are very scary
C runchy snow is chilly and firm
T errible penguins eat lots of fish
I cebergs are as tall as a skyscraper
C old icicles are sharp and pointed.

Latoya Waterfield (6)
Pelsall Village School, Walsall

Snow

S now is as crunchy as crisps
N ice to play in the snow
O utside the snow shines like the sun
W onderful snow falls from the sky.

Grace L (6)
Pelsall Village School, Walsall

Snow

S now falls from the sky
N obody wants to go inside
O h, blow the snow
W inter wonderland.

Jayden Waterfield (5)
Pelsall Village School, Walsall

Ice

I cy, sparkly and shiny
C runching like crisps
E asy to crack and shatter like glass.

April Charmaine Freeman (6)
Pelsall Village School, Walsall

Ice

I cy, sparkling and shining like a diamond
C runching like crisps
E asily cracks and sounds like glass.

Abigail Talbot (6)
Pelsall Village School, Walsall

Ice

I cy, lovely, like diamonds
C runching like crisps under our feet
E asy to crack and shatter like glass.

Joel Humphries (6)
Pelsall Village School, Walsall

Ice

I cy like snow
C runchy like crisps
E verywhere is white.

Addison Stokes (6)
Pelsall Village School, Walsall

Ice

I cy, lovely, like diamonds
C runching like crisps under our feet
E asy to crack and shatter like glass.

Evie-Jane Dickinson (5) & Holly R (6)
Pelsall Village School, Walsall

My First Acrostic – Poems From The Midlands

Hot Wheels

H ow do they stop?
O n the side of the road.
T hey are amazingly fast.

W here does it end?
H ot Wheels are big.
E xtremely exciting.
E nd at the finish line.
L ow engine doesn't win.
S low cars go to the fixer.

Mohamed Ahmed (6)
Robin Hood Primary School, Birmingham

Football

F ootball is the best sport in the world
O n Sunday I will go outside to play football
O n a school day I will show off my skills
T oday is the perfect day to play football
B est sport is football
A black and white ball is a football
L ots of people for football
L ove football because it is fun!

Jannat Choudhury (6)
Robin Hood Primary School, Birmingham

Musa Ahmed

M ust listen to the teacher
U nderstand what teacher says
S chool is nice
A t school do golden time

A t golden time I play
H elpful to other children
M eet my friends
E verybody is nice
D o right and be right at school.

Musa Ahmed (6)
Robin Hood Primary School, Birmingham

Zulekha

Z ig-zag paths
U nder the tree
L ovely potatoes
E xtremely good at art
K ind and helpful
H ate to play in the garden
A dventurous.

Zulekha Nasir (6)
Robin Hood Primary School, Birmingham

My First Acrostic – Poems From The Midlands

Abdulhadi

A t school it is very fun
B eautiful name
D ad is great
U sually very kind
L ovely mum too

H appy all the time
A nd always working hard
D oing work is fun
I am very smiley.

Abdul Hadi (5)
Robin Hood Primary School, Birmingham

Caitlyn

C an play tig
A superstar
I love to be creative
T he house is clean
L ike smiling
Y ou are good
N ew Elsa doll.

Caitlyn Oliver (6)
Robin Hood Primary School, Birmingham

Rocket

R acing out into space
O ut toy zooming out in space
C ats might be there too
K icking canon balls, zooming on and on
E ggs for you as well
T his enormous thing.

Inaaya Nawaz (6)
Robin Hood Primary School, Birmingham

Pragna

P ink is my favourite colour
R eads loudly and writes neatly
A mazing at art
G entle and kind
N ice and helpful
A wesome at study.

Pragna Emani (6)
Robin Hood Primary School, Birmingham

Morgan

M e and my sister never peek at hide-and-seek
O ut in the garden
R oaring noises
G iggling Morgan
A nd it was a flash
N ever scared!

Morgan Simpson (6)
Robin Hood Primary School, Birmingham

Willow

W illow tree is like my name
I like it
L ike a tree
L ovely hair
O h so cool
W ill I stay like this forever?

Willow Powell (6)
Robin Hood Primary School, Birmingham

Summer

S ome days I go to the park on the swings
U nder my bed to play
M y sister Kasey is funny
M y mummy and daddy work
E very day I have toast
R eally big daddy.

Summer Jones (6)
Robin Hood Primary School, Birmingham

Hamzah

H amzah likes Mummy's cooking
A nd he watches non-fiction
M y favourite toy is Thomas toy
Z zz . . . does read at night
A nd he likes his free book
H appy when he is nice.

M Hamzah Qasim Alavi (6)
Robin Hood Primary School, Birmingham

Alisha

A lisha is very kind
I like this school
L ovely lessons to learn
S pecial friends to play with
H elpful teachers
A lisha loves phonics.

Alisha Ali (6)
Robin Hood Primary School, Birmingham

Haniah

H er hair is incredibly long
A t 3:05 we go home
N ever late in the morning
I n at 8:45
A t ten it is my friend's birthday
H er arms are long.

Haniah Azad (6)
Robin Hood Primary School, Birmingham

Aayah

A m happy all the time
A friend comes to play with me
Y ou and me are friends
A t home time I see my mum, she is my friend
H er name is Selina.

Aayah Rafique (6)
Robin Hood Primary School, Birmingham

Kinza

K ind and helpful
I nteresting stories
N ever misses school
Z aggy wearing
A lways good.

Kinza Ibrahmi (6)
Robin Hood Primary School, Birmingham

Henry

H appy
E xtra nice
N ew comic
R eally good at karate
Y ou are a superstar.

Henry Howard (5)
Robin Hood Primary School, Birmingham

Jerry

J elly is wiggly
E ggs are cracking
R ice juice is my favourite
R ipping doesn't make sense
Y eti is the best.

Jerry Zhang (6)
Robin Hood Primary School, Birmingham

Hanaa

H anaa is my name and Ahmad is my surname
A lways share toys
N ice, kind and friendly
A lways don't snatch or pull
A nd always be good!

Hanaa Ahmad (6)
Robin Hood Primary School, Birmingham

Zymal

Z ebras are beautiful
Y ou and I are best friends
M y friends like to play with me
A t school, me and my friends play
L ovely games.

Zymal Rehman (6)
Robin Hood Primary School, Birmingham

My First Acrostic – Poems From The Midlands

Keira

K eep caring, keep sharing
E xtremely nice teacher
I like school
R eading is good
A t home time we go home.

Keira Brazier (6)
Robin Hood Primary School, Birmingham

Hamza

H elpful to his mummy
A lways funny
M assively good at maths
Z ig-zag walking
A mazingly good at art.

Hamza Rahman (6)
Robin Hood Primary School, Birmingham

Pavan

P erfect person
A lways like orange and my favourite colour is pink
V ery clean
A nd I really like my friends
N o one is mean to me.

Pavan Chane (6)
Robin Hood Primary School, Birmingham

Dante

D ante
A mazing at riding my bike
N ice and kind
T alk all the time
E xtremely good.

Dante Nathaniel Pooler (6)
Robin Hood Primary School, Birmingham

My First Acrostic – Poems From The Midlands

Laila

L aila is my name
A ly is my teddy bear's name, he likes to jump
I like to run fast
L ove her style, do you like it?
A ly is my friend.

Laila Galloway (6)
Robin Hood Primary School, Birmingham

Asher

A lways cheeky
S andy beach is my favourite, I run around full of
H ot energy because I eat
E ggs: scrambled – and I
R eally help my mum.

Asher Phansi (6)
Robin Hood Primary School, Birmingham

Sami

S miley
A lways like my friends
M y name is nice
I 've got so many friends.

Sami Ahmad Anjam (6)
Robin Hood Primary School, Birmingham

Umar

U mar is me
M y friends are great
A re you good like me?
R ead good like me?

Umar Ahmed (6)
Robin Hood Primary School, Birmingham

Sara

S he is very tall
A nd she has lovely friends
R eally she is six years old
A nd she has lovely manners.

Sara Kayani (6)
Robin Hood Primary School, Birmingham

My First Acrostic – Poems From The Midlands

Toys

T o play with them
O n fun days playing
Y ou can play with a yo-yo
S onic games are fun playing.

Ibrahim Hussain (5)
Robin Hood Primary School, Birmingham

Qiam

Q uick at running
I n sports football is the best
A t home I am good
M y dad is the best!

Qiam Aariz Jamil (5)
Robin Hood Primary School, Birmingham

Lily

L ittle
I ncredible
L ovely
Y ippee!

Lily Hamilton (5)
St Christopher Primary School, Coventry

Chanel

C areful
H ero
A princess
N ew
E xcellent
L ucky.

Chanel Marie Martin (5)
St Christopher Primary School, Coventry

Rachel

R acing
A ct
C ool
H eart
E xcited
L ovely!

Rachel Butterworth (6)
St Christopher Primary School, Coventry

Hannah

H appy
A wesome
N ice
N oisy
A nnoying
H ungry.

Hannah Elizabeth Nicholls (5)
St Christopher Primary School, Coventry

Eloise

E xcited
L ovely
O ne stamp
I nto exploring
S uper
E xtra amazing!

Eloise Heggie (6)
St Christopher Primary School, Coventry

Reggie

R ays
E xtremely
G ood
G igs and antics
I nteresting
E xtraordinary.

Reggie Jones (5)
St Christopher Primary School, Coventry

Cohen

C ool
O nly one
H ard work
E xcited
N ice.

Cohen Lily-Mae George (6)
St Christopher Primary School, Coventry

Ebony

E gg
B est
O bstacle
N oisy
Y ippee!

Ebony Hanney (5)
St Christopher Primary School, Coventry

Leyna

L ovely
E xcellent
Y oung
M iss
A mazing!

Leyna Yeoman (5)
St Christopher Primary School, Coventry

Carta

C ool
A ct
R ace
T rail
A ssume.

Carta Edward Galvin (6)
St Christopher Primary School, Coventry

Poppy

P roblems
O bstacles
P erfect
P ips
Y ippee!

Poppy Eva Tegerdine (6)
St Christopher Primary School, Coventry

Freya

F antastic
R ight
E verything
Y oung
A dding a sentence.

Freya Davies (5)
St Christopher Primary School, Coventry

Emma

E mma is six
M ammal
M agical
A mazing girl.

Emma Hall
St Christopher Primary School, Coventry

Charlie

C harlie is my name
H ats are my favourite thing
A snake is my favourite toy
R obots are my toys
L ike to play
I am a boy
E ggs are my favourite.

Charlie Servando (6)
St Francis Xavier Catholic Primary School, Oldbury

Harriet

H arriet is my name
A lways kind
R unning I am good at
R ed is my favourite colour
I am good
E ating cake I like
T ea I eat.

Harriet Moore (6)
St Francis Xavier Catholic Primary School, Oldbury

My First Acrostic – Poems From The Midlands

Jasmine

J asmine is my name
A pples I like to eat
S ummer is the time I like to play
M aria is my friend
I like cake
N ever bad
E ating strawberries I like.

Sorrel Hackett (7)
St Francis Xavier Catholic Primary School, Oldbury

Amelie

A melie is my name
M onday is my favourite day
E veryone likes me
L ike to be kind
I am important
E ager and excellent.

Amelie Hemmingway
St Francis Xavier Catholic Primary School, Oldbury

Daniel

D aniel is my name
A good boy
N ice to teachers
I like to play
E very day I feel sad and happy
L ike to run.

Daniel Hurst
St Francis Xavier Catholic Primary School, Oldbury

Macca

M acca is my name
A lways good
C an do gymnastics
C an be noisy
A friend of mine is Paddy.

Macca Ros-Nalugon (6)
St Francis Xavier Catholic Primary School, Oldbury

Izaak

I zaak is my name
Z ebras are my favourite animal
A ll of us stick together
A ll of us are friends
K indness is good.

Izaak Ian Baillie (6)
St Francis Xavier Catholic Primary School, Oldbury

Jacob

J acob is my name
A pples I like to eat
C ats I have at home
O ranges I like
B est at running.

Jacob Iezzi
St Francis Xavier Catholic Primary School, Oldbury

Lacey

L acey is my name
A good girl
C lever Lacey
E at chocolate
Y ou are my friend.

Lacey Evans-Withers
St Francis Xavier Catholic Primary School, Oldbury

Flynn

F lynn is my name
L ike my friends
Y ou are nice
N ice to my friend
N eat work.

Flynn Judge (6)
St Francis Xavier Catholic Primary School, Oldbury

My First Acrostic – Poems From The Midlands

Alex

A lex
L oving
E xcellent
X box.

Alex Whitehouse
St Francis Xavier Catholic Primary School, Oldbury

Anna

A nna is my name
N ice to my friends
N ever like to be bad
A lways friendly.

Anna
St Francis Xavier Catholic Primary School, Oldbury

Lily

L ily is my name
I like to play
L ike to be friends
Y ou are my friends.

Lily Rose Marshall (6)
St Francis Xavier Catholic Primary School, Oldbury

Kaja

K aja is my name
A mazing at running
J am I like
A pples I like to eat.

Kaja Roche
St Francis Xavier Catholic Primary School, Oldbury

Ali

A ll
L ittle
I mportant.

Ali
St Francis Xavier Catholic Primary School, Oldbury

Autumn

A utumn is the time of year that leaves fall off the trees
U nderground animals are hibernating like bears
T o celebrate the Houses of Parliament not getting blown up
we have Bonfire Night
U p in the sky birds are finding food to gobble up
M emories of me jumping up and down in verse
N ight-time animals like owls come out as well as moles, bats
and moths.

Rosa Hickinson (7)
Stanion CE Primary School, Kettering

Summer

S un shines like lava
U mbrellas not used in summer
M y mum pushed me into the Dead Sea
M y dad goes swimming with me
E very summer at the airport going on holiday
R ed if you don't like summer.

Cobi Maddox (6)
Stanion CE Primary School, Kettering

Spring

S pring plants grow
P retty flowers grow
I love spring
R oses grow
N ow we can go to the beach
G o and play.

Sasha Maita Badza (5)
Stanion CE Primary School, Kettering

Minibeast

M oths flutter
I nsects are all around
N ature is beautiful
I nterest in nature
B utterflies are beautiful
E arwigs are all scuttling
A nts
S piders are creepy
T iny beasts run around.

Cerys Neal (7)
Uppingham CE Primary School, Oakham

Minibeast

M unch, munch goes the caterpillar
I nsects are different colours
N ature is quite noisy!
I n and out go some butterflies
B ees are buzzing all around the hive
E arthworms are glowing
A nts are very black
S cary spiders slowly crawl
T iny insects are flying.

Anna Williams (6)
Uppingham CE Primary School, Oakham

Dinosaur

D inosaurs have sharp teeth
I n museums you can see them
N o dinosaurs alive
O ut of the mouths – roar!
S harp claws to dig with
A nd nests for baby dinosaurs
U nderstanding about dinosaurs is fun
R aging tyrannosaurus is silly!

Lexi Scott (6)
Uppingham CE Primary School, Oakham

Minibeast

M umbling bees in the hive making honey
I nteresting moths looking like butterflies
N ice butterflies around me
I nsects always are in and out
B eetles in the trees, yuck!
E arthworms in the thick mud
A nts crawling round and around
S limy, long worms
T iny taps from an ant.

Lexi Foster (6)
Uppingham CE Primary School, Oakham

Dinosaur

D inosaurs are dead
I n the museums there are fossils
N o more dinosaurs anywhere
O mnivores, herbivores or carnivores
S tegosaurus had a brain in its tummy
A re the dinosaurs big enough?
U nbelievable dinosaurs
R acing dinosaurs – stegosaurus wins!

Rian Nitesh Punja (5)
Uppingham CE Primary School, Oakham

Minibeast

M oths are flying
I nsects are under logs
N ests in the trees
I n and out go the butterflies
B ees collecting honey
E arwigs are hiding in the grass
A mazing ants
S low coach worms
T iny lady bugs.

Katelyn Purdy (6)
Uppingham CE Primary School, Oakham

Dinosaur

D inosaurs can be dangerous, deadly and delightful
I n the forest you might find them
N ever feed a dinosaur
O range and brown with massive,
S harp teeth
A nd omnivores are strong and fierce
U nderneath dark, muddy caves you will find them
R aging and roaring and fighting with claws.

Millie Rose Jasmine Tookey (6)
Uppingham CE Primary School, Oakham

Minibeast

M oths flying
I n and out worms
N ests in the ground
I nsects move
B ees asleep
E arthworms wiggling
A nts getting food
S limy snails and slugs
T iny stick insects crawling.

Alexia Grace Whitehead (6)
Uppingham CE Primary School, Oakham

Dinosaur

D inosaurs are enormous
I n museums are bones
N o more dinosaurs around
O n dinosaurs is skin
S tegosaurus is a dinosaur
A nklyosaurus is a herbivore
U nderstanding dinosaurs is awesome
R oar, I am T-rex.

Maisie Draper (6)
Uppingham CE Primary School, Oakham

My First Acrostic – Poems From The Midlands

Minibeast

M umble, mumble go the bees in the hive
I nsects are around you and me
N ature's shield bugs are crawling on leaves
I ncredible dragonfly comes to me
B ees make honey
E arthworms are like worms
A nts are very tiny
S piders have eight legs
T rees are some insects' habitat.

Emily Hathaway (6)
Uppingham CE Primary School, Oakham

Dinosaur

D inosaurs are deadly and dangerous.
I n museums you will find them.
N o more dinosaurs around.
O mnivores, herbivores and carnivores.
S tegosaurus has plates.
A llosaurus is a carnivore.
U nderstanding dinosaurs is great!
R oar, Allosaurus is coming to get you.

Luke Billam (5) Deighton & Leah
Uppingham CE Primary School, Oakham

Minibeast

M inibeasts creep and crawl
I nsects live here and there
N oisy bees buzzing
I ncredible moths
B eware of the spiders
E vil wasps
A mazing worms
S ilent centipedes
T hin stick insects.

Joseph Stacey (7)
Uppingham CE Primary School, Oakham

Dinosaur

D inosaurs are strong
I n museums there are bones
N o more dinosaurs
O mnivores eat meat and vegetables
S tegosaurus just eats vegetables
A ll dinosaurs are scaly
U gly dinosaurs are funny
R oar!

Chloe Sheehan (5)
Uppingham CE Primary School, Oakham

Minibeast

M inibeasts crawling
I mpressive minibeasts
N esting bugs
I n and out insects
B ees buzzing
E arthworms digging
A nts all around
S piders catching flies
T iny bugs in the grass.

Riley Richardson (6)
Uppingham CE Primary School, Oakham

Dinosaur

D inosaurs, sharp teeth, roar
I n museums dinosaurs
N o fit condition young and
O ld fossils, bony, huge
S harp horns to poke with
A mean herbivore, extinct
U sually fossil dinosaurs
R oaring, smelly, gigantic.

Candy Zheng (6)
Uppingham CE Primary School, Oakham

Minibeast

M umbling bees in the hive
I nteresting butterflies in the blue sky
N atural bugs in the grass
I nteresting bugs in the trees
B eetles crawling everywhere
E arthworms rolling into little balls
A mazing bees buzzing
S cary spiders in the dark
T errific bugs everywhere.

Olivia Benson (7)
Uppingham CE Primary School, Oakham

Dinosaur

D inosaurs have sharp teeth
I guanadons run fast
N o dinosaurs alive, extinct
O n the mountains dinosaur feet
S ome dinosaurs eat dinosaur plants
A T-rex is coming to eat me
U h-oh!
R oar!

Bella Banfield (5)
Uppingham CE Primary School, Oakham

My First Acrostic – Poems From The Midlands

Minibeast

M inibeasts – the best
I nsects crawling
N ice bees
I don't like spiders
B ees buzzing
E arthworms slithering
A nts are moving
S ack of honey
T rees are hiding insects.

Charlie Burgess (6)
Uppingham CE Primary School, Oakham

Dinosaur

D inosaurs are extinct
I n museums you can see them
N o more dinosaurs
din **O** saurs are bony
S ome dinosaurs are fast, some are slow
dinos **A** urs are mean
dinosa **U** rs are sometimes
R oar! T-rex is coming to get you!

Scarlett Revitt (5)
Uppingham CE Primary School, Oakham

137

Minibeast

M umble, mumble the bees say
I n and out go the ants to get fruit
N arrow tunnels that ants make
I ncredible bees making honey
B usy bees making honey
E xcellent earthworms squiggling
A pples and pears the ants get
S lugs slither
T reetops are where butterflies rest.

Amelia Jolly (6)
Uppingham CE Primary School, Oakham

Dinosaur

D inosaurs are really dangerous
I love the T-rex
N o more dinosaurs because they are extinct
O h my goodness!
S ame as again, no more dinosaurs
A ny dinosaurs left?
U nderstand, no more left
R unning dinosaurs, walking dinosaurs.

Tia Nikia Pagan (5)
Uppingham CE Primary School, Oakham

Dinosaur

D angerous
I n museums
N o dinosaurs
O mnivores
S harp teeth
A T-rex could eat you
U nderstand no more
R oar.

Grace Quirke (5)
Uppingham CE Primary School, Oakham

Fletcher

F is for fell
L is for low
E is for Ellie
T is for toe
C is for cool dude
H is for hose
E is for enormous
R is for road.

Fletcher Dalby (5)
Uppingham CE Primary School, Oakham

Dinosaur

D inosaur coming to get me
I have to run fast but I
N eed help because I am
O ne and I am a baby, so
S cary, T-rex is going to get me
A rgh!
U h-oh
R oar!

Evie Barnes (5)
Uppingham CE Primary School, Oakham

Dinosaur

D inosaurs are dead
I n their time dinosaurs were strong
N o dinosaurs, young or old
din **O** saurs are bony
S ome dinosaurs are fast or slow
A ll dinosaurs are mean
U nless they are herbivores
R oar! Dinosaurs are dangerous.

Eden Lount (5)
Uppingham CE Primary School, Oakham

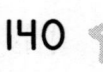

My First Acrostic – Poems From The Midlands

Demi-Lee

D is for my dog, Marley
E is for excited
M is for Mummy
I is for Imogen
L is for love Nanny
E is for Elmer
E is for egg.

Demi-Lee Lambert (4)
Uppingham CE Primary School, Oakham

Joshua

J is for Joshua
O is for orange
S is for Spider-Man
H is for helpful
U is for Uppingham
A is for apple.

Joshua Burgess (4)
Uppingham CE Primary School, Oakham

Maisie

M is for monkey
A is for apple
I is for insect
S is for sausage
I is for impossible
E is for egg.

Maisie Richardson (4)
Uppingham CE Primary School, Oakham

Imogen

I is for I'm cute
M is for mazing
O is for one fairy
G is for girl
E is for excellent
N is for nice and handy.

Imogen Grace Smith (5)
Uppingham CE Primary School, Oakham

My First Acrostic – Poems From The Midlands

Brooke

B is for brave
R is for ready
O is for obvious
O is for octopus
K is for kind
E is for everybody's friend.

Brooke Nugent (4)
Uppingham CE Primary School, Oakham

Thomas

T is for tidy
H is for happy
O is for office on top
M is for mushed up
A is for awesome
S is for special.

Thomas Williams (4)
Uppingham CE Primary School, Oakham

Sofia

S is for snowflakes
O is for on top of the climbing frame
F is for five
I is for in school
A is for alligator.

Sofia Taylor (5)
Uppingham CE Primary School, Oakham

Harry

H is for helping people
A is for action figures
R is for robots
R is for (w)recking stuff
Y is for yak.

Harrison Garrill (5)
Uppingham CE Primary School, Oakham

My First Acrostic – Poems From The Midlands

Elise

E is for egg
L is for Lexi, my sister
I is for insect
S is for special
E is for exciting.

Elise Foster (4)
Uppingham CE Primary School, Oakham

Faith

F is for flower
A is for apple
I is for ice lolly
T is for Thomas
H is for happy.

Faith Young (4)
Uppingham CE Primary School, Oakham

Noah

N is for nice
O is for on top of a tree
A is for amazing
H is for happy.

Noah Hopkinson (4)
Uppingham CE Primary School, Oakham

Rosa

R is for royal
O is for octopus
S is for singing
A is for apple.

Rosa Williams (4)
Uppingham CE Primary School, Oakham

Eden

E is for Eden
D is for dancing
E is for everybody
N is for nice and naughty.

Eden Grace Isabella Tookey (4)
Uppingham CE Primary School, Oakham

Zac

Z is for zany
A is for amazing
C is for crazy!

Zac Dumford-Finnemore (5)
Uppingham CE Primary School, Oakham

Ben

B urgers are my favourite food
E very day is fun for me
N ice to my sisters.

Benjamin Williams (4)
Uppingham CE Primary School, Oakham

Victor

V aluable
I nnocent
C aring
T all
O riginal
R esponsible.

Victor Joseph
Yew Tree Community School, Birmingham

Saarrah Begum

S weet
A dventurous
A dorable
R eally hard working
R espectful
A lert
H elpful
B ubbly
E nergetic
G enerous
U nderstanding
M onster.

Saarrah Begum (6)
Yew Tree Community School, Birmingham

Sahil

S uper star
A mazing
H appy
I ncredible
L oud speaking.

Sahil Ahmed
Yew Tree Community School, Birmingham

My First Acrostic – Poems From The Midlands

Abdul Malik

A mazing
B ehaved
D eep and doting
U nique
L ucky

M arvellous and magical
A rticulate and amusing
L ively
I ncredible
K ind.

Abdul Malik Mohammed
Yew Tree Community School, Birmingham

Subhaan

S port is what I like to play
U mbrellas keep me dry in the rain
B atman is my favourite
H ats and gloves keep you warm
A pples are yummy and tasty, they make my body strong
A fter school I play on my laptop
N odding to one of my friends in my class 1C.

Subhaan Akram
Yew Tree Community School, Birmingham

China

C hina, where you eat with chopsticks!
H amsters eat some whole . . .
O nomatopoeia – *bong!*
P oetry
S tew is so disgusting
T owers are hard to climb
I ce is freezing
C ows are easy to milk
K ings are hard to beat
S low people are always last!

Mohammed Mursalin (7)
Yew Tree Community School, Birmingham

Nabila

N ice
A mazing
B eautiful
I ncredible
L ooking at the teacher
A dventurous.

Nabila Rizwan
Yew Tree Community School, Birmingham

My First Acrostic – Poems From The Midlands

Young Writers Information

We hope you have enjoyed reading this book – and that you will continue to in the coming years.

If you're a young writer who enjoys reading and creative writing, or the parent of an enthusiastic poet or story writer, do visit our website **www.youngwriters.co.uk**. Here you will find free competitions, workshops and games, as well as recommended reads, a poetry glossary and our blog.

If you would like to order further copies of this book, or any of our other titles, then please give us a call or visit **www.youngwriters.co.uk**.

Young Writers,
Remus House,
Coltsfoot Drive,
Peterborough
PE2 9BF.
(01733) 890066 / 898110
info@youngwriters.co.uk